SECOND STORY BOOKS

Mastering the Dream

Kelly Lydick

ISBN 0-9773823-1-1

Portions of this work appeared previously in the
New College Review,
http://www.newcollege.edu/review/lydick.htm

A special thanks to those
who have contributed to this text:

Rabbi Michael Shapiro, Eden Daniel Pearlstein,
Alison Luterman, Brian Teare,
Neeli Cherkovski, Sarah Stone,
Marcus Husk, Sarah Brock,
and my parents,
for their undying encouragement.

Design: Mary Burger.
Cover image: Dwarf Elliptical Galaxy M32,
courtesy of the Hubble Space Telescope
Heritage Image Project.

Second Story Books: Oakland CA

Past	Present	Future
Solid	Liquid	Gas

ש

September, 2005

And the next thing I know, I'm lying on a sterile table, saran wrap between my body and the black vinyl, my arm out to the side, getting inked: Aleph, Mem, Shin: *yesternight* on the interior of my right bicep, and I wonder how I got here.

On the next table, there's another Jew getting an eagle on her back and she tells me the story of another other Jew and how the other other Jew's parents threatened to have her tattoos cut out of her skin before she'd be buried. Hopefully, I think, for their sakes, the parents of the other other Jew will die before the other other Jew and what difference will it make then anyway?

Shin, Mem, Aleph: thesis, antithesis, synthesis; the three original letters.

The girl asks me if I plan to be buried and I tell her: "No, I'm being cremated," and she says to me: "Then you have nothing to worry about." But I am worried. I'm wondering how I got here. And I am alone.

Dear Marie,

It's been a long time since I've seen you. Where have you been? A couple of years back I looked for you in my sock drawer and I found only old fortunes from a dozen different Chinese dinners. One time I even looked for you in the bathtub, but all I saw was a murky reflection and some dead skin sticking to the rubber flowers that help you keep from slipping when you take a shower.

I left you a message awhile back but I thought you knew my voice, so I didn't leave the number. Maybe I should have. The more I know you, the more I realize I owe you, and the more I owe you the more I realize that I love you.

Love, Marie

Septemer, 2005

Every morning when I get out of the shower, I dry myself: left arm, left leg, right leg, right arm, like a circle, and then I meditate: thesis, antithesis, synthesis.

Aleph, Mem, Shin.

Then I look at the freckles on my body. None of the freckles make constellations. I stand naked before the mirror, a map of the stars in my left hand. Technically, it is a fallacy to try to look for constellations on my body, because the mirror shows only the reverse image.

Shin. Mem. Aleph.

April 4, 1998: 10:07 p.m.

This drug is not a necco wafer. It is invisible. It is a lot like god entering my mouth. God the invisible. God the everywhere. God the everything and nothing. This is the invisible. This drug is not a necco wafer, not confectioner's sugar. Poison. Prison.

April 4, 1998: 10:08 p.m.

There is nothing happening. This is invisible. My mouth knows no shame.

The Rabbi says: The mouth is a house of prayer.

April 5, 1998: 1:49 a.m.

This is not happening. This film, this reel, is trapped behind glass. The man on the television is a writer, holes up in the wintertime, tink, tink, tink, typewriter until boredom sets in. He plays racquetball in the living room, Alps outside. Then tink, tink, tink, tink. Too quiet, he is. This reel is not happening.

Tink.
Tink.

All writing and no thinking makes dull stories.
All writing and no thinking makes dull stories.
All writing and no thinking makes dull stories.
All writing and no thinking makes dull stories.
All writing and no thinking makes dull stories.
All writing and no thinking makes dull stories.
All writing and no thinking makes dull stories.
All writing and no thinking makes dull stories.

All reel and no real makes dull characters.

April 5, 1998: 3:36 a.m.

Be my angel. Does he want to be? My angel. He is. He has to be. Who else is he? There's no one here in this room with us and I am dying. What happened when he turned out the lights? Everything got fuzzy and shaky and I waited for the bell to ring, to wake us up so we could go hiking in the mountains.

But the bell never rang and I am shaking and he's my angel and I see him clearly, and he sees me, eyes rolling into the back of my head and now it's light. The light's on. Did he flick the switch? What an angel he is. He knew I needed light and I didn't even have to ask. He knew all along, and I am shaking.

How much time has passed? Where am I now? I can't leave now. I have too much work to do. I can't leave now, and now it's he and I, my angel and he is holding me up from under my armpits, letting the ice cold water hit my face.

It's hours later. It has to be and he is holding me up from under the arms and now I see the gray tile of the shower and now I see his face clearly and death has passed and we are in a cold shower. Now he stays up all night to watch me breathe.

The Rabbi says: Chaos outside, chaos inside.

Dear Marie,

Was I right? Did you make it through the night? You're afraid not to fall asleep, but more afraid to close your eyes. Will you wake up in the morning? Maybe God's angry with you. Maybe God has given up on you because you almost destroyed yourself. Are you frightened?

Tell me what it felt like when you thought your body was collapsing and shutting down. Tell me what it feels like for nothing but your brain to be alive. Falling? Skydiving? Tingling and numb? That's how I imagine it: tingling and numb and then: darkness. I bet you were frightened. Is that why you sweat at night?

Love, Marie

Dream:

i wore the inside out. shirt showed wear. clinging to ribs, breasts, underarms. i want to be the shirt clinging and i do not want to be the shirt clinging. a darkened stain. a useful blood saturated in what i cannot remember. i lose a baby. leave the womb. wonder. wound. wonder. wince. wonder. i want to begin again. cling to myself. master the dream. play god with it. remember.

The Rabbi says: If there's one thing the Earth can do to you, it's create forgetfulness.

Dear Marie,

Do you remember sleeping? You must have at some point. You woke up today, didn't you? I told you you'd wake up. It's like time passed and never passed and now everything is brand new and you're different. You are further away from any tingling than you'd ever imagine you could be.

Have you written it down yet? I know how much you like to write. Do you remember any of your first poems? I have one that you gave to me. Do you remember this one? I always liked it.

South of Beaufort Sea

Coal black
eyes of night
rest upon ants that
make mountains of solace
attempting to build empires
from dust.

Love, Marie

April 5, 1998: 3:03 a.m.

The film is over. It is quiet. It is like the entire world outside this room has disappeared. I am not tired but he wants to go to sleep. We shuffle toward the bed and I am aware of the vast space of darkness. It is as if the world could swallow me.

We lie down shoulder to shoulder, only a sheet covering us. After a few minutes I am sinking. The bed is swallowing me whole. Everything sinks slowly, my body begins to lose feeling. I wake him up, tell him that something is wrong. It's hard for me to breathe. My lungs are collapsing. I have no feeling in my limbs. What's happening? Is my body disappearing? Where did he go? I can't see him anymore.

Dear Marie,

I hear you've started sleeping with a night light. Don't be ashamed. You're never too old to sleep with a night light. Trying to fall asleep with the TV on might be even better. Scientists have done studies on people who live alone and keep the TV on for extended periods of time. It makes people feel like another person is there in the room with them. Not so alone. They say it has calming effects. Is being alone what scares you? Or is it trying to fall asleep in the darkness that makes you toss?

I can see how it might be the dark. And the silence. It was pitch black and silent when it happened, wasn't it? When your body collapsed? I'm sorry. I hate to know that you're so frightened every night. Try the TV. It should help.

Love, Marie

Dream:

hospital room with Mother. two doors on each end of the room. lights off and television on. president and vice president killed. stay indoors. stay indoors. stay indoors. it isn't safe out there. stay indoors. i open mine to the desert. rain and cacti. thought i heard a knock but no one was there.

Dear Marie,

Episodes of syndicated *Honeymooners* and *I Love Lucy*, huh? You know all the episodes by heart, too. Maybe I gave you bad advice. Even with the TV on, your mind still races. Maybe if you didn't know what was going to happen after the conveyor belt of chocolates speeds up? Or maybe if you didn't know that Ralph was going to say: "To the moon, Alice!" Maybe if you didn't know, it would hold your attention and quiet your mind.

How many thoughts do you think the human mind is capable of simultaneously? I think it must be a thousand. Or more. Maybe people aren't even aware of how many thoughts they have at a time because they're having them all at once. The thoughts collide with each other then. Meld into one. Maybe all these thoughts are benign. Maybe they don't mean anything.

I suppose you could try changing the channel. Old shows are nice because you watched them as a child, but maybe something new would be nicer. Promise me you'll get some sleep.

Love, Marie

Yesternight.

April 5, 1998: 12:03 p.m.

The morning after, we eat pancakes and sausage at a restaurant. I don't know which restaurant, but I know the walls are yellow and the table is a thick wood with knots. I say nothing. Can hardly force myself to eat. I am surprised that I am breathing. The entire world looks different and I will never be able to see the old world again. He asks me if I want whipped cream and I tell him that the blueberries and strawberries and bananas and raspberries on top are enough. He kindly pays the bill, rubs the side of my arm and watches my tears fall. I try to hide my face from the waitress, but we leave because eventually there are too many tears, and it becomes embarrassing. Secretly, he is nauseated. I realize it when we walk through the parking lot to his car. I get into the blue Volkswagen and wait, while he stands outside vomiting onto the asphalt.

April 5, 1998: 3:38 p.m.

Hiking is out of the question. We lie in bed, all day, silent. A few times I cry. A few times stifle loud wails and rub my eyes into the pillow. We do what we want, when we want. Right now I want nothing more than to erase the night before. I am disappointed that the world looks different forever.

May 17, 1998

How many times did I look over my shoulder today? Maybe it's because I'm from Chicago. Everyone there jokes about the over-the-shoulder syndrome. It can't be because I'm simply not at ease.

Will I be able to sleep tonight? Will I sweat? Wake up screaming? I'm almost an adult now. There's no one under my bed or in my closet. It will just be me, alone, waiting to fall asleep.

The Rabbi says: Beautiful eyes see beautiful things.

June 23, 1998: 2:07 p.m.

We pushed the limit. He is here and I am here and we are here together. I think of the Volkswagen bug, the knots on the wooden breakfast table, but this is not the same.

We are here in a bed of redwoods and nothing in the world smells the same. The path takes us deeper into the forest. We are pushing the limits. I tell myself: I can do this again and still breathe. The path opens to a meadow. We hear the snap of the bumblebee's wings. I can see the vapor of the clouds, moving, morphing, into anything I want.

This time, we climb to the top of the mountain. It starts to rain; my heart is beating strong. I breathe and he reads to me, "Howl". The gods respond with drops of rain. This time, my heart beats strongly. This time, I sleep through the night.

January, 1999

I am in the Seattle airport. The trip has been cut short due to a weather advisory. I concentrate on the patterned carpet; intersecting diamonds, red, orange. It hides the dirt well. I wonder how many thousands of people walk through this airport on a daily basis. Maybe it's comparable to the number of thoughts that the human mind is capable of having all at once. Or fewer.

He is here and I know this is the last time I will see him for a long while. We sit down on the floor, cover the red and orange diamonds with our butts. I am surprised that he cries a little, surprised that his sadness is overt, his affection at times the opposite.

I agree with him; it's a good idea that I leave early. Now we don't have to push any limits, he won't have to keep watch over my breath. Now I will be alone. I think of the cold shower, reading "Howl." This time, I'm not worried.

מ

April, 2000

An impulse tattoo is like buying a pack of chewing gum at the grocery checkout. This time it's Florida, spring break, my best friend and I. Our birthdays are two days apart and we are almost like the same person. We giggle the same way. I know what she is thinking with just a look.

We want a tattoo that's meaningful, something that displays the bond of our friendship. We decide on our shared astrological sign, the Gemini. It's a roman numeral two, with a slight curve at the ends of the top two lines. We step into a dirty tattoo parlor. I wonder about hepatitis, but try to forget I thought about it in the first place.

The booth is small and cleaner than the front lobby. Our artist keeps pictures of colorful airbrushed naked ladies on the walls. Castor and Pollux would be proud.

We choose a place on the back of our necks and I get nervous and go first. Our artist doesn't use a template, inks freehand and it's unnerving. I can't see until he's done. I wonder if he's creating the right design because I don't want to walk around with the wrong design until I die. I am also afraid that the airbrushed naked ladies could create a distraction, cause a fluctuation in the consistency of the ink.

When it's over, the artist hands me a mirror. Everything looks okay, simply backwards.

May, 2000

I was six years old when I discovered that light was both a particle and a wave. I was lying in the grass on the far side of the creek that ran behind my parent's house in Chicago.

I wanted to see if I could catch the particles. I tried but failed.

May 14, 2000: 3:14 p.m.

My mother sends me an email today: suffering comes from recognizing the discrepancy between reality and your initial vision. My vision is what I thought was there. My vision is what was not there. My suffering is realizing what was not there.

June, 2000

I am looking at a map of the Northern Hemisphere and I can see the twins, Castor and Pollux. I am one and I am also the other. They are, together, nothing but space between a couple of dots. I wonder how long it will be until one of the dots dies and I am left to choose which twin I will have to become.

Dear Marie,

I found another old poem of yours that I think you might like to hear again. Some say it's too abstract, that the idea could be applied to anything, but the entirety still makes sense:

In Hiding

In a multitude of chaos
I am swept, a giant hairball, onto the
world's configuration
of a dustpan.

My barber is a murderer
in disguise.

Love, Marie

Dream:

woman with a black leather purse. bumps me on the way into the store. says i tainted her leather. yelling and i yell back. spit on the leather. stomp it into the dirt wasting five hundred dollars. on a purse. i yell again. enter the boutique. neon lights and jewel cases. music for the customers. fake plastic pink and orange rings. outside tsunami breaks. i pay no heed. drive through the wave. leave the windshield wipers off.

Dear Marie,

It's too black and white. Remember when I told you to sleep with the television on? I said it because you need to loosen your mind. Let it go a bit.

I bought you something. Try keeping this journal. Write things down. Maybe make a list of opposites first and see if it helps you to disintegrate them. Then later you can move on to something else.

Aside: Any good late-night episodes on? Try to avoid *The Twilight Zone*. It might keep you up.

Love, Marie

Black	White
Hot	Cold
Love	Hate
Either	Or
Ignorance	Arrogance
Day	Night
Kindness	Strictness
Yes	No
Consciousness	Unconsciousness
Gain	Loss

Dream:

i am in the garage. figurines on a metal shelf. bird. girl. mouse. elephant. i am supposed to go camping, find the camping gear, but there is nothing on the shelf but bird, girl, mouse, elephant. i am supposed to go camping and everyone is concerned because it's bear season. i am not concerned. i say: it's my car. i say: i am not the bear. i say: i am the bear.

acquire. consummate. gain. conserve.
sustain. lose. forfeit. misplace. forget.

The Rabbi says: It is a great commandment from God to be in joy. Always.

Dream:

mannequins in the warehouse. corrugated sheet metal. i run but they are watching with their empty brains. bald and naked. blue eyes and fake eyelash-es. guilt and fake hearts. and the closet. piled high in dirty clothes. never enough time. forgotten coat. fading scent of cologne. something like a backyard that burns. but this one i don't. weave a wig so the limbs bend better.

ignorant. modest. confident. haughty.
overbearing. conceited. arrogant.

July, 2000

I'm surprised that I go out as much as I do. I'm proud of myself. Now's the time when I work the job and make it through the day. It's a good thing that I can wear headphones while I work. Listen to anything I want. Beatles. Radiohead. Beethoven. At least I don't have to talk much. Explain myself. Keystroke after keystroke, I don't have to think about anything except: shift, tab, type, next, shift, tab, type, next.

They like me here, too. I'm fast. Faster than others. I'm such a good worker. Every boss I've ever had said that I was a keeper.

Solid	Liquid	Gas
Thesis	Antithesis	Synthesis

August, 2000

The brain cannot distinguish between what it sees and what it remembers. What I see is a freckle on the inside of my left middle finger. Another one between the web of my index and middle finger, and another, faintly above my lip.

I wonder if they will still be there tomorrow when I wake up in the morning, or if I will simply remember them. Sometimes it's a surprise when new freckles appear and I wonder if they have been there forever, but only now am I noticing.

The Rabbi says: If you live on presumption alone,
you have sadness coming.

aleph. mem. shin.

August, 2000

There we stood. The male lions and he and I with nothing between but a chain link fence. It reminds me of the kind I used to hop in the alleyways of Chicago to the neighbor's pool on a hot, humid summer day.

This one looks wobbly. There's a crack between the ragged bottom and the dust of the desert ground. A big enough crack that a medium-sized dog could squeeze through. A terrier.

We stand, he and I, looking beyond the fence, trying to see where the male lion has gone, but he's not there. A few minutes pass and then he roars. Have you ever been close to a lion while it roars? It makes your hair stand up on your skin and when the wind blows against your arms all of the sudden you remember you're alive. I think to myself how easy it would be for this lion to diminish my existence into nothing. Two seconds it could take. Maybe three.

I wish I had a tape recorder so I could capture the sound, play it back every morning, a reminder of what it means to breathe.

chest. water. hot. thesis. belly. air. head.
synthesis. heart. receptivity. fire. antithesis.
creativity. chest. water. hot. thesis. belly. air.
head. synthesis.

September, 2000

I am on the train and I listen to a sad song about fixing things that are broken. Irreplaceable. I think: there are thoughts that are irreplaceable. I think: there are moments that are irreplaceable. I think: there are a few moments that I would like to replace permanently:

1. the memory of the Seattle airport carpeting
2. a recent argument with my best friend
3. the sound of the bumblebee's wings in the forest

March 18, 2001: 7:18 p.m.

I enlarge the font on my mother's email that says: suffering comes from recognizing the discrepancy between reality and your initial vision. I print it out and tape it to the wall, next to the mirror above my bureau.

either. and. or.

The Rabbi says: Your ability to love is found in your ability to pay attention.

Dear Marie,

Remember this:

You are in seventh grade. You've already eaten lunch. You're in a science classroom. Geology; you've chosen it this quarter. You always liked rocks.

You are hovering over a shoebox on a black formica table. The tables are black because they don't show wear or burn marks. There are different types of rocks in one shoebox, concentrated elements in another.

mica, calcite, quartz

sulfur, calcium, iron filings

The same filings used to make Wooly Willy. You know them by heart with a glance. Chip is your partner. You always want to be Chip's partner because he smiles a lot. You are real friends. There's nothing written on the blackboard. You smile at each other.

Love, Marie

March, 2001

This one, he's different. I find it strange that he has a roman numeral two in the same place that my best friend and I do. Maybe it's just a coincidence.

He asks me if I like science, reminds me that yes, I do. I say: "There's nothing more fascinating than time and space." I think he finds this reply inspiring.

Later on another occasion, I confide in him that I can see light particles, that as a child, I knew light was both a particle and a wave. I've never told this to anyone before, and I'm not sure why I do now.

Maybe I think he'll understand. Maybe I secretly hope that he can see the same thing, too.

Dear Marie,

You think to yourself now: science. When did I forget? Math was easy; writing difficult. Do you remember passing out of all of your college math classes in high school? Do you remember being in danger of failing English?

You had a math brain.

You always liked rocks.

Love, Marie

She writes a story about two boys who spend an entire summer looking for a hidden fallout shelter underneath a library in rural Nebraska. Charlie and Dodie. Patterson Library at the intersection of Main and Orange. Irish librarian. The boys look for cracks, loosening planks, pretend to read books and avoid being discovered. Pretend to be magicians to turn each other into inanimate objects that could talk. Hysterical laughter. Kites, baked beans, a pair of red glasses, a bat, playground swings.

Then one day Charlie, alone, finds the fallout shelter, climbs all the way down, and when he returns, he finds the entire town destroyed. Nuclear bomb. Some timing. But not really because she's the writer and she planned it that way. Charlie never had any choice.

Dear Marie,

Here it is again. I'm sorry but you need to remember:

Seventh grade. It's after lunch. Chip your partner has missed two consecutive weeks of school. You miss him. Class begins and there are no shoeboxes on the black formica tables. The tables are bare, roll hasn't even been called, and then: it is announced it over the loudspeaker as if it were the pledge.

Chip died that morning.

That afternoon, Chip had become invisible, too.

Love, Marie

August, 2001

This time it is my choice to leave, and I leave despite that I love him. I leave to go and write, write this, write anything. I wonder if it's the end for us and it kills me inside. It's like I'm hyperventilating all the time.

Somehow I am reminded of the Seattle airport. Somehow I am reminded again that I love science. I wish, somehow, that I could make the knot in my chest disappear.

I look in the sock drawer and read a fortune from a Chinese dinner:

"Your current plans will be successful."

She writes a story about a man who seals his lover up behind a white brick wall. It is the same as Edgar Allan Poe, but different. This time, in this story, the man and woman make love, and the man resents the woman. He holds a gun to her head. Neither of them know whether it's loaded, but like to pretend it is.

They are pushing their limits. It's amusing to test mortality. When they finish, he locks her hands together, seals her up behind his bedroom wall so that at night he can hear her moaning, haunting him.

scalding. scorching. hot. warm. lukewarm.
tepid. cool. cold. frigid.

October, 2001

Can a mausoleum smell like freezer burn? This one does. Except for the back room in the corner with the fountain and the blue mosaic tiles arranged on the wall. That rooms smells like pancakes and sausage. Better than freezer burn, bitter.

Each room in the mausoleum has been given a different name: Patience, Trust. I trust that this room is supposed to remind me of my own mortality, but it doesn't. Concrete pillars, ionic replicas not smoothed down. When I run my fingers over them I can feel the bumps in the concrete running counter to the ridges of my fingertips. It feels good. Fingertip to whole palm, fingertip to wrist. And it reminds me of the things I miss.

She writes a story about her old lover. She disguises herself in a character and tries not to disguise him. Tries to expose him as best as she can. She makes the girl character ask: "When I'm over, will you find a way to keep me alive somehow?" But then she realizes that if the dialogue for the girl character is made up, then the dialogue for the real lover has to be made up too, else she would end up with dialogue something like:

"When I'm over, will you still keep me alive somehow?"

"I'd rather have chicken tonight."

So she scraps the story because after the girl character says: "...somehow?" she can't really think of any response that the old lover could believably say.

The Rabbi says: Information is not knowledge.

א

February, 2006

Old concepts of the world are broken down in our minds by only 0.1% of the construct of reality we have created for ourselves.

This morning when I looked in the mirror I couldn't see myself. Or any of my freckles. Gravity has finally pulled its own weight. Libra, Castor, Pollux, Gemini have disappeared. They are part of the 99.9% space.

My identity is part of the 0.1% of matter.

With a marker, I try to trace the shape of my body onto the mirror. Mostly it's correct because of how I remember myself, but some of it has changed because of what I can't see now.

I try to meditate, Aleph, Mem, Shin, but it's difficult to do looking only at the ink on the mirror instead of my body.

Marie writes a story about two lovers in a futuristic world where touch is outlawed. The grandmother makes tea, tries to warn her granddaughter. Grocery. Silver, metallic, inhuman. Fruit stand. That was where they met. Be careful making change. Don't touch the cashier. Be careful making change.

Eventually the lovers are running from the city. They end up in a field beneath a pile of stars. The man points out the constellations to the woman. Her grandmother would be disappointed.

The man and woman kiss and turn to dust. Maybe it's because on this planet the laws of physics are different.

The cycle is king in the domain of time.

Yesterknight.

Dear Marie,

You should remember this one too:

In a math class one day, you decided to use a ball point pen to connect your freckles, like a child's connect-the-dots game. You got as far as both arms before a teacher forced you to go to the restroom and wash yourself.

Love, Marie

February, 2006

This morning I invented a recording device that worked as a reminder, that could record your voice, and then after setting an alarm, the reminder would play back to you what you needed to remember.

It would work really well because the voice would be your own voice. It would feel authentic, and the reminder would be valid. That way I could remember to do specific things at specific times, or not forget specific things like balancing my checkbook or my uncle's birthday. Or the time of the next lunar eclipse.

Marie writes a story about a young boy and girl. It is the Vietnam War. It is Roe versus Wade. It is the women's liberation movement.

The boy's father is a war hero. The girl's family is dysfunctional. The neighbor lady dies and leaves behind her pet mice. The boy and girl kidnap the orphaned mice and release them into a field. The boy and girl kiss.

love. admire. like. estrange. dislike.
abhor. detest. despise. hate.

June, 2006

I am in Florence, Italy. It has been three and a half weeks. I stand on a bridge overlooking the Arno River. This is the moment that I realize how tiny my body is compared to the Earth. This is the moment that I realize I am on the other side of the Earth. This is the moment I realize my life is but a speck of dust, a flickering star in a distant constellation, a freckle on someone's arm. There is never really any loss or any gain, I am here and I am alone while completely surrounded, and the world looks different forever.

July, 2006

I am in a vehicle driving on a deserted road in Southern Italy. I am sandwiched in the back seat between two other people. We are driving to an old castle that has been turned into a dance club. There are no street lights. There are no reflectors dividing the lanes.

I look at the blue neon light on the face of the cellular phone. My hands start to clench. I am clammy. My palms sweat and my eyes can't focus. The road is not straight. I am shaking and my hands are clamped, tighter now. My shoulders tense and my teeth chatter. Soon I can't open my palms. I can't hear anything.

And the next thing I know, I wake up in an Italian hospital. A doctor is measuring the peaks and valleys on a piece of graph paper that is supposed to represent the beats of my heart. I do not understand all that he says, but he's not worried. He knows how I got here. He tells me in Italian: "It's all in your mind."

Dream:

doctor's house all day. orange walls and stethoscopes. poker game with high stakes. MD, OD, Ph.D. one of them interprets my dream, asks me about miniature salt packets. checks my blood pressure. i recommend reading over epic television shows.

The Rabbi says: If there's one thing the Earth can do to you, it's create forgetfulness.

Shin	Mem	Aleph
Past	Present	Future

August, 2006

I am on an airplane going to Las Vegas. We are flying through a desert storm and the sky is black. It's lucky that I'm sitting next to a doctor.

I hyperventilate into the white bag that was stored in my seat pouch when the flight began. I think I might have a heart attack.

I turn to the doctor and ask: "What happens when someone has a heart attack in the middle of an airplane flight?" He says: "They usually land the plane." I wonder about the times when they don't land the plane.

He assures me I am not having a heart attack. I look at the placard, read the instructions on how to make the seat cushion a life vest, try to laugh.

Dear Marie,

Do you ever wonder if the things that define us are the exact things that hold us, oppress us, keep us stuck? I think every time you say "I am" you're also saying "I'm not". Does this make sense?

Here's a poem for you:

Titanium

Put on your hip boots.
Lace them tightly,
if you can.
When the wading is done
perhaps we can have
a conversation,
say the things we
meant to say and haven't
never did I
have
been meaning
to tell you
the mud has gotten thicker, dried out.
Maybe if you tread heavily
it will crack, open up
swallow you and
me and allow only
an echo to remain

a wave,
a particle,
an electron,

we may as well share it
we are already sharing the cloud.

Love, Marie

aware. cognizant. bemused. vacant.
insensate. paralyzed. unaware.

Dream:

babysitter and six kids. break into the neighbor's house to eat cookies with rainbow sprinkles. cages of rare and endangered animals. cheetah morphs into polar bear, lion beasty, unknown species. "this is a spectator sport, look around," someone says. zombies.

sunrise. morning. day. afternoon. evening.
twilight. dusk. nightfall. night.

Marie writes a story about a girl who keeps getting freckles. Not sun damage, new freckles. The girl connects them all together with an ink pen.

Every freckle on the girl's body is a new story—every spot a memory. There are some freckles that she wishes she could erase. Remove from her body permanently. There are some freckles the girl reveres.

Then, the girl meets a boy. He asks her to tell him the stories her freckles hold. Mostly she tells them all, but leaves out the story of the evening she almost dies. That freckle is located on the top of her foot.

Years ago she would have told him. He would have wondered why she couldn't sleep at night. Now it's irrelevant. In fact, maybe the girl never died that night at all.

The Rabbi says: The brain cannot distinguish between what it sees and what it remembers.

November 11, 2006: 12:48 p.m.

I take down the printed version of my mother's email that says: suffering comes from recognizing the discrepancy between reality and your initial vision. I crumple it up into a ball and throw it in the trash.

Dear Marie,

Remember this?

You are in graduate school. You are becoming a writer. The teacher praises you on your conceptual work. You need improvement in prose.

Then, in a poetry class you write a paper on Sylvia Plath. You choose her because you know all about her tragic life and nothing of her work. Perhaps there's a correlation between the two that you'd like to discover?

You study her star chart. Her sun is in Scorpio, like your moon, and this scares you. You find it unnerving. Do you remember asking yourself whether there's a correlation between Plath and yourself? Is the minute similarity enough to make you dislike cooking? Poetry? Never mind. Maybe there's nothing to discover about it.

Love, Marie

Dream:

everest. i climb out of the water. unchoppy. handles. i am wearing shoes. look up and out to snow caps. all the makeup has been thrown away. rolled under the vehicle and smashed. i am glad for my bare face. calm water. orange. dusk.

November, 2006

This morning I invented a pill that tastes like turkey dinner with cranberry, that fills you up, without making you sleepy, so that everyone can stay awake enough on the holidays to have sex before they go to bed, so everyone will have something to say thanks for.

Then I invented a pill that cures heartbreak so that everyone suffering from heartbreak, whose capillaries were full and pulsing with blood, will know exactly what blood to send and where. That way the love-blood, at least for a time, would be sent not to the heart and head but to the feet, because the feet are the farthest from the heart.

Then I invented a post-heartbreak pill that insanely makes you go out and repeat the same process again.

Turkey and cranberry.
Heartbreak.
Post-heartbreak.
Turkey and cranberry.

Then I really got creative. I invented a pill that makes me remember all the important parts about my life that I've forgotten, like:

1. my first birthday party
2. winning the fifth-grade spelling bee
3. the shape of my childhood friend Chip's smile
4. the way my father taught me to ride a bike

But then I thought: what if the remembering pill reminded me of moments I'd like to forget?

1. killing a robin with the neighborhood kids at age six
2. my first kiss at age twelve
3. the way my grandfather looked the night before he died
4. being held under a cold shower after almost dying
5. the look on my first love's face when he left me at the airport
6. the things my mother said to me after I got my second tattoo

I un-invented that one.

Marie writes a story about a woman who, in a past life, was a Spanish Jew. The woman is a writer, has problems fully expressing herself. She secretly knows she was a Jew, but never knows how that life ended. Never knows that in that life, she was a man.

Against the 613 mitzvot, the woman approaches a seer, finds that she was a man, learns that he was persecuted for writing, quartered and burned. Maybe, the woman thinks, this is the reason why writing is the most difficult destiny.

Later, the woman travels to Spain, searches out every synagogue, at all ends of the countryside, for the place where her last life ended. No luck.

As the women makes her way back to the city, she inadvertently stumbles over the place, in the stable of a dairy farm, where a man is milking a cow. Surprising, the woman thinks, that such cows could be at such peace in a place of violence.

The man in the stable tells her: "No farm I've ever worked on had cows that produced as much milk."

Dream:

i am the barber.

December, 2006

Is it possible to forget yourself more than once? And if you forget do you cease to exist? Maybe the memory of self is all in the mind. Maybe it's only an amalgamation of thoughts—a thousand thoughts all at once. Can you murder thoughts? Can you cremate thoughts? Sweep them all up? Let them turn to dust?

Maybe cremated thoughts are like disintegrated opposites. Maybe you have to murder the Either/Or to get the And.

March, 2007

I write a novel about three friends who have known each other for years. One is a sculptor, one a salesman, and one a scientist. My characters remind me of a modern version of *The Three Stooges*.

The three have many adventures, traverse the country in search of an answer to a mysterious shellac. Why are people dying? the three wonder. And what does the shellac have to do with it?

By the end of the novel, the three expose a greedy corporation for committing environmental injustices. The book sells millions of copies.

black. an underground cave. a dark room.
the clouds before a thunderstorm. the shingles on
a roof. static on the television. the softly shaded
sections of a charcoal figure drawing. the exterior
casing of a 1980's boom box. the metal chains on a
playground swingset. a doctor's labcoat. white.

Dear Marie,

This is the last reminder you'll be getting:
Love is like a memory, a true joy, the only source. It is never lost nor gained, nor absolute, there is nothing to remember or forget.

Don't you remember what you've said? All the aphorisms you've given me throughout the years? My favorite is: Beautiful eyes see beautiful things.

Aside, I've found one of your poems in my sock drawer. I'm sure you'll remember it.

Paddleboat

Without need for wind,
two-by-two
our feet
smitten to muscle
of calf and shin,
when we awake
it is like awake
            again
awake again
it is like you
like me.

Drifts drift,
but impossible with tooth
and pedal

impeccably hooked
me
in
rote but constantly
anew
this flap
impregnates water,
flippant,
berated.

Pedal and tooth
driving
a drill through shell
a cut into stone
a ripple into water
to make sound lapping
at the side of you
curled into the side of
me,
we lay like
we sit
and steer
as if water
were endless and
quenching.

Love, Marie

kind. benevolent. cordial. withheld.
disciplined. stern. malevolent.

July 7, 2008: 2:47 p.m.

My mother sends me an email today:

Be mindful of your thoughts as they become your words.
Be mindful of your words as they become your actions.
Be mindful of your actions as they become your habits.
Be mindful of your habits as they become your character.
Be mindful of your character as it becomes your destiny.

Dear Marie,

I knew you could do it. Master the dream. Maybe all those sleepless nights weren't in vain. Maybe now you'll sleep better.

Do me a favor—remember what the Rabbi said.

Love, Marie

Dream:

the world is flat. every constellation is above. i see them all. i see northern and southern hemispheres. the twins have faces. the kite is flying, nestled between a scorpion and a virgin. my life is like all the space between the stars. i see for the first time. everything is clear. the bear is not chasing anything.

Shin	Mem	Aleph
Past	Present	Future
Solid	Liquid	Gas
Thesis	Antithesis	Synthesis

In Memory of Charles Nelson

Afterword

The concepts put forth in *Mastering the Dream* are based in Jewish mysticism; however, I do not claim to be a scholar in Judaism, nor do I claim that *Mastering the Dream* encompasses all of the potential meanings or interpretations that Jewish mystics or scholars have explored. I myself am a student and not an authority, constantly pooling new information into my bank of knowledge, and constantly ready to renew the conclusions my mind has come to. In addition, I am not attempting through the text to teach these concepts, but rather to put the character in direct conversation with the ideas I've represented. I've chosen to attempt this through an abstract narrative, within the form itself. The nature of the work is not meant to be a linear narrative, but something that can be strung together in various combinations of components.

The Hebrew letters Aleph, Mem, Shin (אמש) which appear in *Mastering the Dream* spell *Emesh*, which means *yesternight*, a word that's found in Genesis. According to some mystics, and later analyzed by scholars, these characters comprise what are known as the three "mother letters." They are outlined as such by Aryeh Kaplan in his translation and interpretation of the *Sefer Yetzirah*, or *The Book of Creation*. As the "mother letters," these characters are the very first letters, and the very first symbols from which all matter has sprung and from which all forms of life (visible or invisible) can be constructed.

From these three letters, all the other letters of the Hebrew alphabet can be derived, and can in various forms describe all matter in the universe. In *Mastering the Dream*, this idea is represented through reference to the solid, liquid, and gas states of matter.

The letters Aleph, Mem, and Shin contain many layers of symbolism; in totality, they represent everything in our physical and spiritual worlds. The letters also have individual meanings, referred to in *Mastering the Dream*:

> Shin (ש)is a representation of the concept of a thesis (original inception or idea), the element of fire, and on the physical body, the head;
> Mem (מ)is a representation of antithesis (or idea opposing the original thesis, Shin), the element of water, and on the physical body, the belly;
> Aleph (א)is a representation of synthesis (the blending of thesis and antithesis to produce a new, different, higher form; the blending of Shin and Mem), the element of air, and on the physical body, the chest.

The major themes in *Mastering the Dream* are past, present, and future, and the abstract concepts of thesis, antithesis, and synthesis. On a physical plane, thesis and antithesis can represent two opposite directions on a two-dimensional line, and with synthesis create a third point in space and thus the third dimension. A further theme is the belief that every human being is endowed with the power and ability to create—create a work of art, create a meal, create a skyscraper, whatever it is that he or she wishes to create.

On a large scale, *Mastering the Dream* explores the reconciliation of binary opposites, whether in the spiritual world or the physical world, and seeks to represent this reconciliation through different aspects of the narrator's experiences. Marie experiences her past, analyzes it in the present, and creates a future. This concept is also represented by the lists of binary opposites, which are later broken down into gradations. While the abstract application of these concepts is expressed by words and language, or lists, the narrative continues by showing Marie, who changes her life in her future by practically applying what she learned while disintegrating these opposites. The struggle for the character is essentially for her own consciousness to evolve, a process which she believes must include the first step in breaking down the notions that perpetuate binary opposites.

Writing—both the act of writing, and the written text—are also, for the character Marie, the disintegration, or the synthesis, between waking life and dreaming life. Within Hebrew mysticism, waking life comprises approximately 1% of the entire substance of the universe. In a sense, waking life and dreaming life are reversed, as waking life embodies the spiritual challenges we face, and the dormant periods are in their own way the gateway to other "higher worlds."

In *Mastering the Dream*, I've attempted to depict both a conceptual and emotional journey, to put forth the abstract concepts in the *Sefer Yetzirah*, and to create a character that can bring these abstract elements into conversation with an experimental narrative form. After all, if the 1% of reality that we experience here on earth is as fleeting as a dream, why not delve a bit into the other 99%?

— Kelly Lydick, 2007

Notes

Page 14: "The mouth is a house of prayer." Eden Daniel Pearlstein. Olympia, Washington. www.myspace.com/eprhyme.

Page 17: "Chaos outside, Chaos inside." Rabbi Michael Shapiro. *Divine Order*. Compact disc audio archive #545. Scottsdale, Arizona: Scottsdale Torah Institute and Center for Spiritual Growth (STI).

Pages 20 & 80: "If there's one thing the Earth can do to you, it's create forgetfulness." Rabbi Michael Shapiro. *Reclaim Your Wonder*. Compact disc audio archive #575. STI.

Page 30: "Beautiful eyes see beautiful things." Rabbi Michael Shapiro. *Beautiful Eyes*. Compact disco audio archive #552. STI.

Page 44: "It is a great commandment from God to be in joy. Always." Rabbi Michael Shapiro. *Breaking Your Chains*. Compact disc audio archive #559. STI.

Page 50: "If you live on presumption alone, you have great sadness coming." Rabbi Michael Shapiro. *Expansion*. Compact disc audio archive #546. STI.

Page 57: "Your ability to love is found in your ability to pay attention." Rabbi Michael Shapiro. *Dimensions of Love*. Compact disc audio archive #580. STI.

Page 68: "Information is not knowledge." Albert Einstein.

Page 89: "The brain cannot distinguish between what it sees and what it remembers." Dr. Joe Dispenza. *What the Bleep!? Down the Rabbit Hole*. Captured Light and Lord of the Wind Films, 2004, and Twentieth Century Fox, 2006.

Page 108: Aryeh Kaplan. *Sefer Yetzirah, The Book of Creation*, pages 140-146. Boston: Weiser Books, an imprint of Red Wheel/Weiser, 1997.

Kelly Lydick received her B.A. in Writing and Literature from Burlington College, and her M.A. in Writing and Consciousness from the New College of California. She currently resides in the Bay Area.

Second Story Books publishes new narrative writing by innovative storytellers.
Editor: Mary Burger